Trolls

by Grace Hansen

abdobooks.com

Published by Abdo Kids, a division of ABDO, P.O. Box 398166, Minneapolis, Minnesota 55439.
Copyright © 2023 by Abdo Consulting Group, Inc. International copyrights reserved in all countries.
No part of this book may be reproduced in any form without written permission from the publisher.
Abdo Kids Jumbo™ is a trademark and logo of Abdo Kids.

Printed in the United States of America, North Mankato, Minnesota.

052022

092022

THIS BOOK CONTAINS
RECYCLED MATERIALS

Photo Credits: AP Images, Everette Collection, Getty Images, Shutterstock PREMIER,
©Hey1234 p.22/ CC BY-SA

Production Contributors: Teddy Borth, Jennie Forsberg, Grace Hansen
Design Contributors: Candice Keimig, Pakou Moua

Library of Congress Control Number: 2021950555
Publisher's Cataloging-in-Publication Data

Names: Hansen, Grace, author.

Title: Trolls / by Grace Hansen.

Description: Minneapolis, Minnesota : Abdo Kids, 2023 | Series: World of mythical beings | Includes online
resources and index.

Identifiers: ISBN 9781098261900 (lib. bdg.) | ISBN 9781098262747 (ebook) | ISBN 9781098263164
(Read-to-Me ebook)

Subjects: LCSH: Trolls--Juvenile literature. | Mythical animals--Juvenile literature. | Folklore--Juvenile
literature. | Legends--Juvenile literature.

Classification: DDC 398--dc23

Table of Contents

Myth of the Troll

Long ago, people began telling stories about trolls. The stories come from **Scandinavia**.

The First Trolls

In the 13th century, an **Old Norse** text called *Prose Edda* was written. In it, a character meets an unkind troll woman in a forest. This is one of the first times "troll" was written down.

Bökenn Edda
Hvoria Samsett
Hefur
SNORRE
Sturluson Lög
Madur
Prentud i Kaupenh.
3 Islendsku Dönsku z
Latinu
Anno Domini 1666
hugin
munin
Hamaren Miolner
Clas axen
Heimdall Biallar Horn
Kyrinn Audumla
Sleipn' hefir odinn
Fenris ulfur
Prose Edda

Early stories described trolls as scary and mean. They were very large and strong. Luckily, they were not smart and were easily tricked.

Their arms were long. Their skin was rough and hard, like stone. Some were covered in plants and dirt. This way, the trolls could easily hide.

These trolls lived up in mountains or forests. They sometimes attacked villages and flattened homes. They only came out at night. If sunlight hit them, they turned to stone.

Later Trolls

Later tales told of a far different kind of troll. These trolls were small with round bellies. They had sharp teeth, big noses, and messy hair. Some had tails.

They lived in small **communities**.
These trolls could be found
underground or in caves.

Some myths say that trolls had magical abilities. They could even change how they looked.

Smaller trolls could still be
harmful toward humans. But
tales also tell of them being
helpful. However, they often
expected rewards for their deeds.

Modern Trolls Based on Mythology

Stone Trolls
The Hobbit

- 12 feet (3.6m) tall
- Small head, huge body
- Great strength
- Mean and not smart
- Turned to stone by sunlight

Trolls
Trolls the Movie

- Small with wild hair
- Live in a **community**
- Very cute and happy
- Like to sing and dance

Trolls of the Valley of the Living Rock
Frozen

- Small and stubby with large noses
- Live in a community
- Have magical abilities
- Avoid the sun by turning to stone and burrowing into the ground

Glossary

community – a group of beings that live in the same area.

Old Norse – the Germanic language of Scandinavia before the fourteenth century.

Scandinavia – a region of northern Europe made up of Norway, Sweden, Denmark, and Finland.

Index

Abdo Kids
ONLINE
FREE! ONLINE MULTIMEDIA RESOURCES

Visit **abdokids.com** to access crafts, games, videos, and more!

Use Abdo Kids code
WTK1900
or scan this QR code!